TECHNOWORLD

Computers

Ian Graham

Produced for Hodder Wayland by
Discovery Books Ltd
Unit 3, 37 Watling Street, Leintwardine
Shropshire SY7 0LW, England

First published in 2000 by Hodder Wayland,
an imprint of Hodder Children's Books
This edition published in 2001

ISBN 0 7502 2712 5

A catalogue record for this book is available from
the British Library

Printed and bound in Italy by G. Canale & C.S.p.A.,
Turin

Designer: Ian Winton
Editor: Gianna Williams
Illustrations: Keith Williams, Kevin Maddison

Hodder Children's Books would like to thank Barclays Bank Plc, Boeing Management Company, Boots the
Chemist, Compaq, Epson, Ford Motor Company Ltd, IBM UK Ltd, The Meteorological Office, Microsoft,
NASA, Philips, Safeway, Sega and Singapore Zoo for the kind loan of their material.

All screen shots in this book appear courtesy of the producers of the websites they depict and
remain the copyright of those producers. Every effort has been made to contact the copyright hold-
ers of the screen shots in this book. If any rights have been omitted the publishers apologise and
will rectify this in any subsequent editions.

All trademarks are acknowledged. Apple, the Apple logo, Macintosh, QuickTime and any other Apple
products referenced herein are trademarks of Apple Computer, Inc, registered in the US and other
countries. Eudora is a registered trademark of the University of Illinois Board of Trustees, licensed
to Qualcomm Incorporated. Microsoft, Microsoft Internet Explorer, MSN, and
any other Microsoft products referenced herein are registered trademarks of Microsoft Corporation in the US and other countries. Netscape
Communications Corporation has not authorised, sponsored, endorsed or
approved this publication and is not responsible for its content. Netscape
and the Netscape Communications corporate logos are trademarks of
Netscape Communications Corporation.

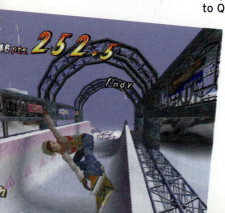

Hodder Children's Books
A division of Hodder Headline Limited
338 Euston Road
London NW1 3BH
England

CONTENTS

COMPUTERS EVERYWHERE

It is almost impossible to do anything without using computers. When you make a telephone call, computers switch the call onto the right line. Products from mobile telephones to airliners are designed and made using computers. Computers create amazing special effects in films and they enable you to play spectacular games.

1. Stop thief!

A burglar steps through a window. A computer sensor fitted to the window detects the burglar's entry. A computer sends a silent signal to the nearest police station.

2. Red alert

At the police station, another computer flashes the house address onto its screen with a message saying that a break-in has been detected.

3. Computers in control

A police patrol car is sent to the house. A computer at the police station records the time the alarm went off, the address of the house and the time the police car investigated it.

The first electronic computers were built in the 1940s in Britain and the United States and they were huge.

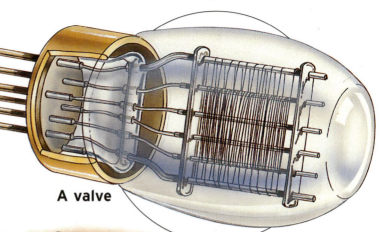

A valve

TECHNOFACT

Cracking codes

One of the first computers ever built was a top-secret machine called Colossus, built in 1943 in England. Colossus was used to decode secret messages sent by German forces during World War II. Colossus had about 1,500 valves.

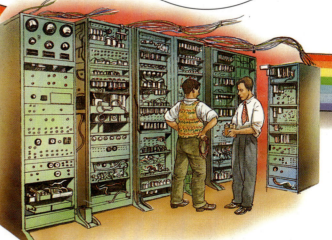

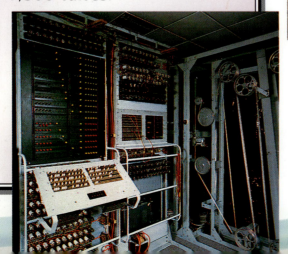

They were made from glass parts called valves or vacuum tubes. Valves switched electric currents, representing numbers, on and off. The valves broke easily. They needed a lot of electricity to work and they were very hot.

Transistors

In 1947 the transistor was invented. A transistor is much smaller than a valve and needs less electricity.

A transistor

▲ ENIAC, a computer built in the USA in 1946, was a giant made from 18,000 valves. It was 24 metres long, more than two metres high and it could do 5,000 calculations per second!

Chips

In the 1950s, microchips were invented. Thousands of transistors could be fitted on one chip the size of a fingernail. Computers today, called PCs, are small enough to fit on a desk or even the palm of your hand.

A microchip

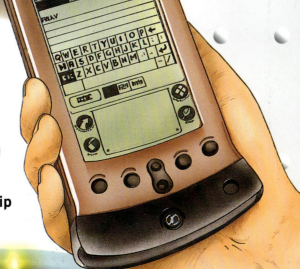

HOW COMPUTERS WORK

Computers take in information, store it, work out problems and then send out answers. They take information in through a keyboard. The information is stored in memory chips or on a hard disk, a floppy disc or a CD-Rom. It is processed by a chip called a microprocessor. Finally, the results are sent to a monitor or a printer.

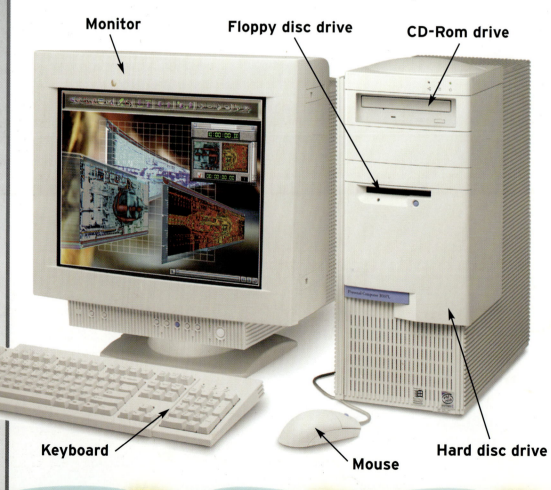

Monitor

Floppy disc drive

CD-Rom drive

Keyboard

Mouse

Hard disc drive

Bits and bytes

The tiniest piece of information a computer can process is a 'bit'. A bit is a number – either a zero or a one. A code made up of eight bits can stand for any letter, number or symbol. Eight bits is also called a byte. Computer memory is measured in millions of bytes, called megabytes, and thousands of megabytes, called gigabytes.

Printer

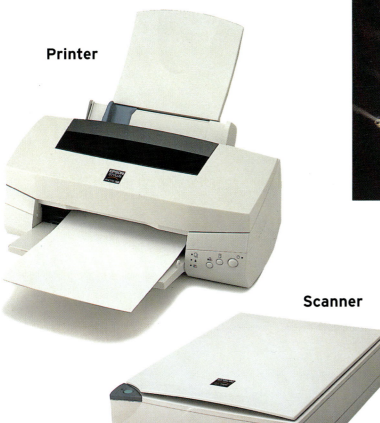

Scanner

Memories

The computer onboard the Apollo 11 spacecraft, which landed the first man on the moon in 1969, had much less power than today's computers. Apollo 11's computer had a 37,000-byte memory. A hand-held computer today has about one megabyte (one million bytes) of memory.

HOW DO COMPUTERS KNOW WHAT TO DO?

A computer is told what to do by sets of instructions, or programs. The programs that tell the computer what to do are called software. Software usually comes on floppy discs or a CD-ROM.

Everything that appears on a computer's screen and the sounds it makes are controlled by a program.

CD-ROMS can hold all sorts of different types of information – text, photographs, sound, computer graphics, animation and video.

A CD-ROM can store about 600 megabytes of data, or a whole encyclopedia on one disc. A DVD-ROM can hold a massive 8.5 gigabytes (thousand megabytes) per side, or 30 times the amount of information in the *Encyclopedia Britannica*.

Books that would take up a whole bookshelf can now be fitted onto a single optical disc.

T E C H N O F A C T

Laser technology

CD-ROMs and DVDs are known as optical discs. Information is stored as pits in the disc's mirror-like surface and read by shining a laser on the disc as it spins.

11

NETWORKS

A group of computers connected together is called a network. Computers send information to each other by telephone. A modem changes the computer data into signals that can be sent down telephone lines. At the other end of the line, another modem changes the signals back into computer data. Messages sent from one computer to another like this are called e-mail.

A small computer network in an office or a building is a Local Area Network (LAN). Computers connected over long distances by telephone make up a Wide Area Network (WAN).

Surfing the Net

The biggest computer network of all is the Internet. Millions of computers all over the world are linked together by telephone to form one giant network. Once connected to the Internet, you can find out information on almost every subject by looking on the World Wide Web.

▲ Using the Internet, people can share information from computers all over the world.

◄ A Web page has written information and can also show pictures, play sounds and even video clips. This is Singapore Zoo's website.

COMPUTERS IN ACTION

Computers know what you buy and where you buy it. Almost every product you buy has a barcode somewhere on it.

When a laser beam shines on the barcode (or 'scans' it), the reflection tells a shop's computer what the product is.

▲ Using the barcode information, the supermarket computer sends the latest prices to the check-out.

The supermarket computer automatically subtracts products sold from the numbers in stock so that fresh orders can be placed.

Credit cards

When customers pay for goods with credit cards or cash cards, the shop's computer reads information stored in the magnetic strip on the back of the card.

▲ Shop computers are linked to bank and credit card company computers so that money can be moved between them.

▶ In some supermarkets, you can scan the barcodes on your own shopping to save time at the check-out.

SUPERCOMPUTERS

Supercomputers are the fastest computers in the world. They are thousands of times faster than a PC. Supercomputers work at such amazing speeds by using thousands of processors, all doing calculations at the same time. PCs are slower because they have only one processor chip.

▶ This Cray-2 supercomputer is being used to develop space-based laser weapons.

Predicting the weather

Weather forecasters use supercomputers to predict how clouds, storms and rain move and change. Scientists use them to study how the tiniest particles of matter behave.

A supercomputer at a meteorological office has worked out weather patterns which are then displayed on PC monitors.

COMPUTER-DRIVEN

Computers are used at every stage of the transport business. Cars, trains, boats and planes are all designed with the help of computer programs called computer-aided design, or CAD, systems. The designs are often tested before vehicles are built by using computer programs.

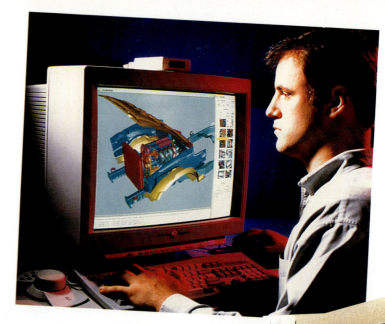

▶ Using CAD to design a new car.

Tests using models and full-size vehicles are studied by computers. Finally, robots controlled by computer can build them. More and more cars today have on-board computers to control their engines.

◀ A car is built by computer-controlled robots.

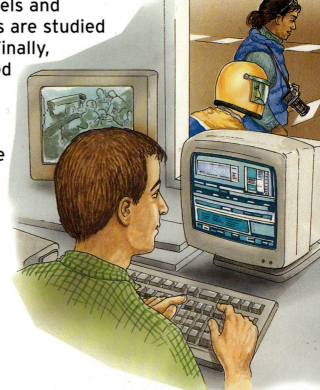

Racing computers

Every Formula 1 racing car has a computer inside its sleek body. It constantly adjusts the engine to keep it running at its best. In addition, sensors all over the car feed information to the computer. The information is sent by radio to the team in the pits, so that they can see exactly how well the whole car is working.

A Formula 1 racing car stops in the pits while being monitored by a computer.

FLYING HIGH

Computers can help fly planes as well as design them. An autopilot is a computer that can control an aeroplane for most of its journey. The pilot only takes over the controls during take-off and landing.

▶ ▲ The Boeing 777 airline was the first plane to be designed entirely by computer.

Air traffic controllers use computers to track aeroplanes in the sky and make sure that they are at safe distances from each other.

◀ Air traffic control computers show where every aeroplane is, with information about its height and destination.

Flight simulators

Airline pilots practise how to deal with any problem that might happen during a flight and they do it without leaving the ground. They sit in a machine that looks like an airliner's cockpit, but it is not a real plane. The view through the window is created by computers, which also move the cockpit so that it feels real.

An airliner's crew is put to the test in a flight simulator. Its computers can reproduce any in-flight fault or emergency.

COMPUTERS AND CRIME

Investigating a major crime involves collecting vast amounts of information about people, places, times and objects. Computers are very good at storing and processing information, so police forces use them to help solve crimes. They can quickly search through hundreds of thousands of words and facts to find names, places, car numbers and so on.

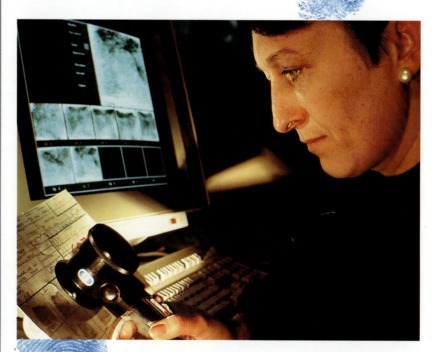

A criminal's fingerprints are scanned into a computer. When fingerprints are found at a crime scene, they can be compared with those in the computer's memory.

Fingerprints and DNA

Computers are also good at comparing patterns, so they are used to match fingerprints taken from a crime scene with fingerprints kept by the police. Police forces have begun to use computers to compare the DNA of a suspect, found in small samples of hair, skin or blood, with DNA found at a crime scene.

Scientists check a sheet of genetic code. Police forces now use computerized DNA checking to help catch criminals.

Computers can create pictures that look like the real world, but they exist nowhere except inside the computer's memory. Called virtual reality, this is a type of computer program that lets you enter a special computer world and move around inside it.

Most virtual reality systems show their pictures on an ordinary computer screen. Immersion systems are different. You wear a headset with video screens in front of your eyes. You feel as if you really are in the middle of the computer's virtual world.

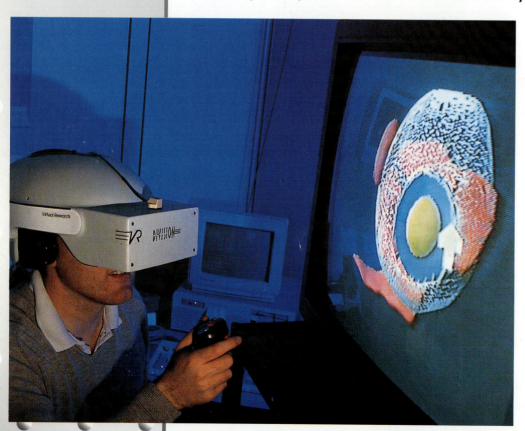

Some surgeons are trained in how to perform new operations by using virtual reality. While the student performs virtual eye surgery, a computer creates a picture of what would be happening on a real eye.

Make-believe buildings

You can now walk through a building before it is built. A computer is programmed with the building's design. The whole building is stored in the computer's memory, but the screen shows one small part of it, as if you were standing in one room. From there, you can move around the rest of the virtual building.

Virtual reality pictures helped prove that this machine would fit in the tunnel specially built for it.

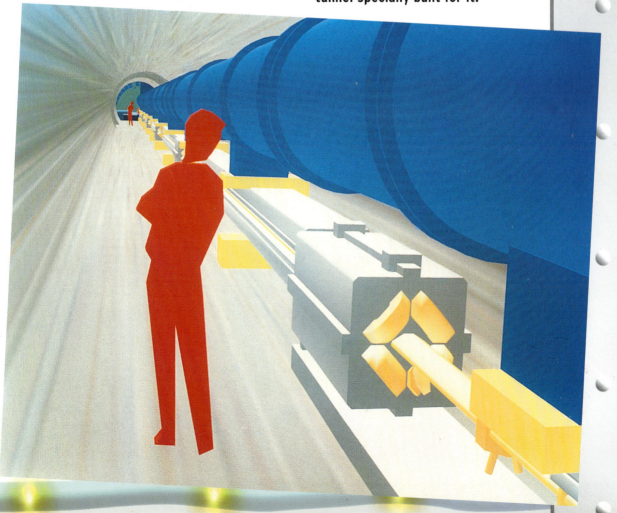

COMPUTER FUN

The first computer games were slow, with few colours and very simple graphics and sounds. Now, thanks to faster processors and much bigger memories, games are quicker, more colourful, more realistic – and more difficult! Their sounds include speech, music and lots of sound effects.

You can race cars or play almost any sport without ever leaving home by plugging specially produced computers and software into a television.

Internet gaming

You can find thousands of games to play on Internet websites. You can try out new games and sometimes you can download (or copy) a game from a website into your own computer. You can even play a game against someone else, linked through the Internet.

There are lots of computer games available on the Internet. Some games can be downloaded free while others can be played online.

27

COMPUTERS IN THE MOVIES

Today computers used in the movies can bring dinosaurs back to life or raise the *Titanic*. The images produced by computers are added later to pictures that were first filmed in the normal way.

Computers created thousands of robot soldiers for the film *Star Wars: Episode 1 The Phantom Menace*. It would have been practically impossible to create an effect like this by drawing each robot by hand.

Computer animation

Computers today can now create entire films. The first film created entirely from computer pictures was called *Tin Toy* in 1994. All the pictures for the films *Toy Story* (1995) and *A Bug's Life* (1998) were computer generated.

The Disney film *Tron*, made in 1982, was the first film that used computer animation. Most of the picture was filmed in the usual way. Then computer graphics were added to create the effect of characters inside a computer game.

GLOSSARY

barcode A pattern of black lines printed on most of the things we buy that can be read by a computerized till or check-out in a shop.

bit A binary digit, a number that can only be 0 or 1.

byte Eight bits, such as 10110011.

CD-ROM Compact Disc Read Only Memory, a type of CD that contains computer data.

code Letters, numbers or signs that stand for information.

DNA Deoxyribonucleic acid. The part of every living cell that contains instructions for creating new cells.

drive Part of a computer that spins a floppy disc, hard disc, CD or DVD so that the computer can read the information recorded on it.

DVD Digital Versatile Disc, a type of CD that can hold all sorts of information, including music, computer data, movies and games.

e-mail Short for 'electronic mail', messages sent from one computer to another using the Internet.

floppy disc A thin magnetic plastic disc that is used to record computer data.

gigabyte One thousand million bytes.

hard disc A stiff magnetic disc, or a set of discs, inside a computer for storing information.

Internet A computer network that stretches around the world.

laser A device that sends out a very powerful beam of pure light.

megabyte One million bytes.

memory The part of a computer where information is stored.

microprocessor A processor that is stored on a single microchip.

processor The part of a computer that works out answers to problems, made up of different microchips.

modem A box that helps to link a computer to a telephone line so that it can communicate with other computers.

mouse A device that, when moved, makes a pointer move in the same way on a computer screen.

program A list of instructions that tells a computer what to do.

ROM Read Only Memory, a type of computer memory that stores programs and information even when the computer is switched off.

sensor A device that changes something like sound, vibration or temperature into an electric current.

supercomputer One of the biggest, fastest and most powerful computers on Earth.

transistor A tiny device used as a switch inside a computer.

vacuum tube A device that computers used to be made from.

valve Another name for a vacuum tube.

virus A small computer program deliberately written to cause damage to computers.

website A collection of pages of information at the same address on the World Wide Web.

World Wide Web A huge library of pages of information stored in computers all over the world, linked together by telephone.

FURTHER READING

Claybourne, Anna and Wallace, Mark, *The Usborne Computer Dictionary*, Usborne, 1999
Coleman, Michael, *Crashing Computers*, Hippo, 1999
Hughes, Lisa, *Computers Unlimited*, Hodder Children's Books, 1998
Maran, Ruth, *Computers Simplified*, IDG Books Worldwide, 1996
Meredith, Susan, *Starting Computers*, Usborne, 1999

Picture acknowledgements:
The publishers would like to thank the following for permission to reproduce their pictures:
6 Science Museum/Science & Society Picture Library, 7 Los Alamos National Laboratory/Science Photo Library,
12 Maximilian Stock Ltd/Science Photo Library, 13 Alberto Incrocci/Image Bank, 16 top Lawrence Migdale/Science
Photo Library, 16 bottom Keith Kent/Science Photo Library, 17 D Muntefering/Image Bank, 20 bottom
B Harringon/The Stock Market, 22 left James King-Holmes/Science Photo Library, 22 right Philippe Plailly/Science
Photo Library, 23 & 24 Hank Morgan/Science Photo Library, 25 David Parker/Science Photo Library,
27 Associated Press/Topham Picture Point, 28 & 29 Corbis/Everett.

INDEX